VANGUARD SERIES

EDITOR: MARTIN WINDROW

ARMOUR OF THE VIETNAM WARS

Text by SIMON DUNSTAN

Colour plates by PETER SARSON
and TONY BRYAN

OSPREY PUBLISHING LONDON

Published in 1985 by
Osprey Publishing Ltd
Member company of the George Philip Group
12–14 Long Acre, London WC2E 9LP

British Library Cataloguing in Publication Data

Dunstan, Simon
Armour of the Vietnam wars. – (Vanguard series; 42)
1. Vietnamese Conflict, 1945–1975 – Tank Warfare
I. Title II. Series
959.704′342 DS559.8.T3

ISBN 0-85045-585-5

Filmset in Great Britain
Printed in Hong Kong

Dedication: To Freddie

Author's note

For those wishing a fuller account of the tactical and technical employment of armour in Vietnam, the reader is recommended the Osprey publication *Vietnam Tracks – Armor in Battle 1945–1975*. The aim of this Vanguard book is to present a pastiche of armoured operations in Vietnam, ranging from single tank exploits through small-unit actions and typical armour missions to full-scale engagements fought by complete armoured formations. To this end, the author has drawn freely on veterans' recollections, after-action reports and published combat accounts, of which the following are gratefully acknowledged:

M113 Mechanized Operations in the Mekong Delta, Bill Bricker and Stanley Holtom, formerly Captains US Army, Advisors to the ARVN, 1962; *Just Another Day in the Corps*, Ken Zitz, formerly Captain USMC, Commander Company B, 1st Tank Battalion, RVN, 1969; *The Battle of Binh An*, Ralph B. Garretson Jr., formerly Major US Army, Commander Troop A, 3rd Squadron, 5th Cavalry, RVN, 1968; *Armor in the Wire*, John Early, formerly Sergeant US Army, Special Forces, RVN, 1968; *Go Seven Blocks and Turn Left*, Nguyen Trung Tanh, from *Giai Phong* ('Liberation').

The author also wishes to express his appreciation to the following individuals and organisations for their invaluable assistance:

Arme Blindée et Cavalerie; *Armor* Magazine; George J. Balin; Col. Raymond R. Battreall Jr.; Geoff Cornish; FMC Corporation; Col. Michel Henry; Col. Stanley E. Holtom; WO Doug Lennox; Col. Bruce M. MacLaren, USMC; Gen. Henri Prèaud; *Soldier of Fortune* Magazine; Col. Gary L. Solis, USMC; 11 Armored Cavalry Regiment; US Army Center of Military History; US Army Military History Institute; *USMC Gazette*; USMC History and Museums Division; Steven J. Zaloga; and Major Ken W. Zitz, USMC.

The standard tank of the French Expeditionary Force at the outset of the campaign was the M5A1; although superseded by the M24 Chaffee from 1950 onwards under the US Military Aid Program, it remained in service throughout the First Indochina War. (Arme Blindée et Cavalerie)

French Armour in Vietnam

In late 1945 the French Expeditionary Force landed in Vietnam with the mission of reoccupying the former colony of Indochina, comprising Tonkin in the north, Annam and Cochinchina in the south and Cambodia and Laos. By mid-1946 this had been achieved with relative ease by armoured units and truck-mounted infantry seizing the major towns and key centres along the country's primitive road network. In December 1946 full-scale hostilities were resumed by the Communist Viet Minh.

During the first phase of active operations up until the end of 1949, the French Army sought repeatedly to engage the Viet Minh in a set-piece battle where its superior firepower could inflict a crushing defeat. In a series of ever-widening envelopments combining paratroop drops and mobile armoured columns, the French extended the war into the hinterland; but the elusive enemy were not to be trapped by such conventional tactics. The Viet Minh resorted to ambushes, interdiction of roads, and the occasional annihilation of outposts.

In response, French armoured units had to assume the mission of route security by the opening of roads, the escort of convoys and the maintaining of lines of communication. Increasingly they acted as 'fire brigades' or reaction forces to come to the aid of besieged outposts or units pinned down in an ambush. Against an enemy who excelled in ambush tactics and who did not hesitate to attack tanks, these missions became increasingly hazardous and required substantial numbers of accompanying infantry. The lack of troops made it impractical for the High Command to permanently assign to the tank battalions their own infantry units, since the infantry would not be used while the armoured units were being refitted or undergoing maintenance. In addition, those infantry units that worked with armour were frequently rotated; so the cohesiveness of the task forces formed under such circumstances suffered, as did the flexibility and rapidity of their operations.

Infantry battalions also required armour support against an enemy who was becoming increasingly better armed and trained. Close co-operation between armour and infantry became necessary, but the latter continued to display the deliberate and slow pace on operations which is their characteristic. In the words of one armour commander: 'The fact was that once an operation began it was pursued at the relatively slow cadence of infantry, and thus appeared in the classic form, familiar since 1918, of infantry combat supported by tanks.'

Moreover, the monotony of repeated operations over the same terrain, together with the long waiting periods associated with safeguarding communications or forming '*bouclages*' (blocking positions), and the wide dispersal of tank squadrons, contributed to an attitude of complacency which led to the static employment of armoured units and to their fragmentation. Due to the lack of resources this fragmentation was often carried to extremes, compounded by the numerous requests for armour support from area commanders at all echelons. This situation adversely affected the effectiveness of armoured units, and caused a high rate of wear and tear on the elderly equipment which maintenance personnel could not redress: not only were they not organised to support so many widely-dispersed detachments but, having only wheeled vehicles, they were confined to roads, as well as suffering from an inadequate supply of spares.

It was not until 1951, after the assumption of command by Gen. de Lattre de Tassigny, that armoured units were reorganised with their own infantry when the first two armoured groups (*sous-groupements blindées* or GBs) were formed. Under the command of a headquarters section, each group comprised one squadron of M24 tanks of four platoons, each with three Chaffees and two half-

'Crabes' of 1er Régiment Étranger de Cavalerie disembark from a landing craft during Operation 'Normandie' in the Plaine des Joncs, June 1950 (ABC)

A remanufactured M4A1 Sherman negotiates a narrow road through dense wooded terrain, ideally suited to ambush, near the Black River during 1951. (ABC)

tracks, and two mechanised infantry companies mounted in half-tracks. The latter lacked the excellent mobility of the M24, with its low ground pressure; but the effectiveness of the new formations was confirmed on operations during 1952.

At the same time amphibious units were expanded. Formed in 1947 using M-29C Weasel amphibian cargo carriers (known to the French as '*crabes*'), these units had proved themselves well-suited to combat in the deltas, swamps and inundated paddyfields of Indochina. Initially employed for supply purposes and later for reconnaissance, the Crabs had initially encountered severe problems – indeed, some of the early operations were complete failures. In the words of one High Command report: 'They were too few in number and were handled by poorly qualified personnel. They thus quickly sowed the Plaine des Joncs [Plain of Reeds] with their burned-out hulls.'

Subsequently the Crabs were manned by the Foreign Legionnaires of the 1er and 2e Escadrons of 1er Régiment Étranger de Cavalerie (1er REC), who developed effective tactics for their employment, and within a short time 'they ranged over the Plain of Reeds sowing confusion in the ranks of the enemy.' The two squadrons formed a '*groupe d'escadrons*' which became the nucleus for '1er Groupement Autonome' created in the south in September 1951. The 2[e] Groupement Autonome was also organised for operations in Tonkin. Each comprised two squadrons with 33 Crabs apiece, divided into three platoons; three Alligator squadrons each of 11 LVTs, which carried three infantry platoons aboard their LVT4s; and a fire support platoon of six LVT(A)4s armed with 75 mm howitzers. The amphibious groups were reorganised in April 1953 for greater flexibility, as were the armoured groups, so by the end of the year French armour in Indochina had the capability to engage the enemy independently and with effectiveness.

Other armoured units included reconnaissance groups (*groupes d'escadrons de reconnaissance* or GERs) each composed of one M24 squadron, an armoured car troop of three platoons each of five M8 armoured cars, and one platoon with three M8 75 mm self-propelled howitzers; armoured car reconnaissance units, made up of two platoons divided into three patrols each with two vehicles, and two platoons of infantry mounted in half-tracks or M3 scout cars; a tank destroyer battalion equipped with M36B2s to counter a possible Chinese tank invasion of Tonkin; and various armour troops manning river patrol boats and *Rafale* ('wind blast') armoured trains.

Although these armoured and amphibious formations were an important part of the French Union Forces in Indochina, their principal manoeuvre elements were mobile strike forces known as *groupement mobiles* or GMs. These were composed of up to three infantry battalions supported by a towed 105 mm artillery battery and a platoon or two of tanks. Being truck-mounted,

An M24 Chaffee fires in support of the Foreign Legion's I/5e Régiment Étranger d'Infanterie near Hoa Binh during the battle of the Black River in 1952. (ABC)

GMs were predominantly roadbound and therefore susceptible to ambushes. The most famous of these was Groupement Mobile 100, which was supported by an entire tank squadron – the 3ᵉ Escadron, 5ᵉ Régiment de Cuirassiers 'Royal-Pologne' (see Plate B2). During the six months of its existence, GM 100 covered almost 2,000 miles through the enemy-dominated Plateaux Montagnards, enduring repeated ambushes at the hands of the Viet Minh 803rd Regiment and others, until it was virtually annihilated only days before the armistice which finally became effective on 1 August 1954. The first Indochina War was over.

ARVN Armour in Vietnam

As part of the Army of the Republic of Vietnam (ARVN), an armoured force was organised in 1956 comprising four armoured cavalry squadrons equipped with obsolescent equipment left by the French. Each squadron had one troop of M24 Chaffees and two reconnaissance troops of M8 armoured cars, M8 self-propelled howitzers and M3 half-tracks. However, the tanks were not employed offensively against the Vietnamese Communists (Viet Cong), although they were used to topple and sustain successive governments in Saigon. For this reason, and because most of their officers were political appointees, armour personnel were known derisively as 'coup troops'. Only the ageless M8 armoured car was used tactically for patrolling, armed escort, and to keep open ground lines of communication.

In April 1962 two mechanised companies were formed of 15 M113 APCs apiece, and on 11 June they were employed operationally for the first time in the Mekong Delta. As in much of SE Asia, terrain 'trafficability' was extremely poor. The limited road network was constantly disrupted by the Viet Cong with demolitions and ditching of roadbeds to deny their use to wheeled vehicles. Bridges were rickety and poorly constructed, and the cultivation of rice kept vast stretches of the land inundated during much of the year. During the dry season, the sunbaked dykes were formidable obstacles. Numerous rivers, canals and drainage ditches cut the countryside, and areas of jungle and mangrove swamp further compounded the problems of mobility.

Troops dismount from an LVT4 Alligator of 1ᵉʳ REC during Operation 'Clavecin' in Cochinchina, March 1952; standard armament of the LVT was two .50cal. and two .30cal. Browning machine guns. (ABC)

The Mekong Delta was the 'rice bowl' of Vietnam and, together with Route 4 to Saigon, of great strategic value. Consequently, the 7th and 21st Mechanised Rifle Companies were deployed to the area to root out the Viet Cong from their formerly inviolable strongholds and to protect the 'Rice Route'. Despite being well versed in conventional armour tactics, having attended the US Army Armor School, most ARVN armour officers had never fought the VC in the field, and they tended to employ the APC merely as a substitute for a heavy truck. Once these problems of doctrine were overcome, the M113s were effectively used as fighting vehicles as opposed to mere transportation to the objective area – as reflected in the following account of a successful operation against the Viet Cong conducted by the 7th Mechanised Rifle Company with 7th ARVN Division in September 1962.

After careful reconnaissance of the area by the unit's US advisor from an L-19 aircraft, the operation began at 0515 hours. Of the 15 APCs assigned to the company, nine were available; of the six not operational, two were deadlined with starter trouble, one had lost all but two bolts in an idler wheel, one was being fitted out as an M132 flamethrower, and two were being used for training at the ARVN Armour School. After picking up three other US advisors the company moved out. At first all went smoothly and movement was rapid. The M113s functioned well until an hour and a half into the march, when one APC lost all but four of its idler wheel bolts (a common defect on early M113s). The rest of the operation narrative is reported through the eyes of the company US advisor:

'We decided to take the vehicle on with us and, consequently, were forced to decrease the march rate. This delay caused the company to cross the LD ten minutes late. I considered this performance remarkable: four months prior to this operation, we would have been lucky to cross the LD at all, much less on time. Punctuality has much less impact upon the thinking of people native to South-East Asia than it does upon the thinking of Americans.

'I kept watching for our L-19 aircraft, which was supposed to be in direct support of the mechanised company. We needed aerial observation to lead us across the flat land, to locate short routes, and to help find suitable crossing sites on the canals. The leading platoon leader was doing a good job of reconnaissance, but the march rate could have been increased if we had the aircraft working with us. Finally, we had to halt and wait for a canal crossing site to be found. My counterpart spotted an observation aircraft and made radio contact, but the aircraft was spotting for fighters and did not have time to help us for very long. The pilot did make two passes and gave us valuable information about the size of the canal and the terrain to our immediate front.

'We continued to move slowly to a point just east of our first objective. Here, two of the three vehicles assigned to the leading platoon bogged down as

M36B2 tank destroyers of the Régiment Blindé Colonial d'Extrême-Orient advance along a road near Son Tay in Tonkin, July 1953; originally deployed to counter possible intervention by Chinese armour, the tank destroyers acted in a fire support rôle. (ABC)

Half-tracks of a mechanised infantry unit deploy over open ground during Operation 'Mouette' near Phu Nho Quan in Tonkin, November 1953; the canvas tilts acted as a shield against both the sun and hand grenades. (ABC)

they tried in vain to cross a small canal. We moved on without this platoon, leaving instructions for them to rejoin the company as quickly as possible. The temporary loss of the three vehicles was reported to higher headquarters. The terrain provided fair visibility now, and we were able to move faster.

'Our mission was changed en route: we were ordered to bypass Objective 1, continue to Objective 2, and block the escape route of a Viet Cong unit along a four-kilometer front marked by a canal. Shortly thereafter, we were ordered to cross this canal and attack a group of some 60 Viet Cong. The ground was firm under our tracks, and the water was crystal clear, with a slight sulphur taste.

'The lead element, under the control of the executive officer, arrived at Objective 2 at approximately 1045 hours. He immediately put out his infantry to locate a crossing site on the canal. Our command track bogged down in a large, well-concealed canal adjacent to a banana grove, and we dismounted to co-ordinate with the executive officer and to reconnoiter on foot.

'There was a well-protected village sprawled along the high ground paralleling the canal. We entered the village on foot. Fortifications about a meter high covered the entrances to the village. Mantraps (bamboo spikes, poisoned nails, etc.) were located throughout the area. On entering the village, we immediately noted that everything was extremely quiet. No adults were to be seen, no children playing – even the dogs were out of sight – a typical situation in Viet Cong territory. We destroyed the mantraps, the fortifications, and the propaganda hut in which the Viet Cong post their propaganda and harangue the villagers.

'An air strike was taking place to the west and south about 2,000 meters from our location. I wanted to observe the air strike, and we had yet to locate a crossing site on the canal to our front. Climbing a large tree which appeared to have been used before, perhaps by a Viet Cong lookout, I found a firm position, and through my binoculars spotted two bushes near the center of the area for use as a reference point. I scanned the area carefully, but saw no indication of the enemy. I covered the area again, scanning carefully. Either the two bushes had moved, or I was feeling the effects of the hot sun. Observing closely, I noted that the two bushes were moving. The movement was carefully co-ordinated with the overflight of a B-26 aircraft which was making an air strike to the south. The bushes moved only after the aircraft had completed its circle and passed over them. Then the shiny metal of a weapon flashed in the sun from one of the bushes, and it was obvious that I was watching two very patient and well-camouflaged members of the Viet Cong. Shortly thereafter, I located 12 more Viet Cong with weapons.

'While I was observing, the executive officer had moved a vehicle up to the canal and asked me to locate a good exit point on the far bank. My vantage point in the tree made it easy to locate a suitable site. Within 15 minutes after selecting the crossing site, the lead vehicle was on the far bank.

'We emplaced the 60 mm mortars, but the enemy apparently had heard us and commenced to shift his position beyond the range of the light mortars. The Viet Cong, whether they were aware of it or not, were completely surrounded by ARVN units

One of the initial batch of M113 APCs to be deployed to Vietnam negotiates a flimsy bridge during the training of the first two mechanised rifle companies in early 1962. (Stanley Holtom)

and had no choice but to fight, hide, or surrender. By now, three APCs had crossed the canal and we decided to attack with one platoon instead of waiting for the entire company. We were in constant communication with higher headquarters and we reported our intention to attack without further delay. (Later, a prisoner told us that the Viet Cong thought we were in boats because the carriers did so much swimming. Based on this erroneous assumption, the enemy had decided to

An armoured unit comprising M24 Chaffees, half-tracks and M8 self-propelled howitzers with supporting trucks and jeeps pauses in the town square at Sept Pagodes during an operation in Tonkin, 1953. (ABC)

attack us. Thus, we had a strong element of surprise of which we were unaware at the moment of decision.)

'Unable to contact our observer in the L-19 circling overhead, we attacked straight ahead toward the point where I had last seen the Viet Cong from my vantage point in the tree. I was riding with the executive officer and I tried – in vain – to get him to move to the flank of the Viet Cong position. We moved rapidly, killing several of the enemy with the .50cal. machine gun when they tried to escape.

M8 armoured cars and an M3 scout car of the Prévôté Militaire (Military Police) patrol the streets of Hanoi after the armistice; these were the last French AFVs to leave what became the Democratic Republic of Vietnam. (ABC)

An M113 of the 7th Mech. Rifle Co. spans a watercourse by means of improvised bridging during one of the first operations in the Mekong Delta. (US Information Service)

'Suddenly, all hell broke loose. Viet Cong appeared all around the APCs. Some were firing automatic weapons; others were firing rifles. Some were running in an effort to evade the tracks. The Vietnamese platoon members fired in all directions from the open hatches.

'At the time, the Viet Cong fire did not seem important to me: I was concerned about friendly fire, which seemed to be coming at us from all directions. The track on which we were riding had a section of bridging on it and we could not take full advantage of the vehicle's armor. The .50cal. machine gun dominated the action.

'Finally, after much effort, I was able to get the troops to dismount. We were still in the middle of a three-ring circus as far as action was concerned, and it was a serious mistake to dismount. As long as we were mounted and moving, the Viet Cong had been unable to fire well-aimed shots. Our mounted positions afforded good observation. We could look and fire down on an enemy who had no effective concealment or cover. Dismounted, we lost our advantageous observation and we could not move rapidly in the knee-deep water. But the Viet Cong knew the terrain despite the fact that it was largely covered with water. They moved on the higher ground of an underwater knoll that stretched across the front, and this gave them a decided advantage. Enemy fire was accurate once we ceased moving rapidly, and we suffered casualties which I believe could have been avoided if we had continued to fight mounted.

'There was a complete lack of squad control. Efforts were largely on an individual basis and there was the appearance of complete disorganisation. The soldiers seemed to have gone mad. On locating a Viet Cong weapon crew, they jumped up and down, shouted, and completely disregarded enemy fire and their own wounded. They were like starving wolves closing in for the kill of a wounded animal. The ARVN pays a high reward, sometimes as much as 10,000 piasters (75 piasters equal one US dollar), for the capture of an automatic weapon. Chances to earn such rewards, plus the excitement of battle, created an almost unbelievable situation.

'After a hectic hour, the fight subsided, and we commenced searching out the Viet Cong who were still hiding in the area. This action was much better organised, but the soldiers still became very excited when they saw one of the enemy, whether he was armed or not. Overhead, the observer in the L-19 continually threw out smoke grenades to mark newly discovered Viet Cong locations. The Viet Cong were still all around us. The CO called for the assistance which we needed to properly search the area. When reinforcements arrived by helicopter, we evacuated our wounded and the Viet Cong prisoners and conducted a well-organised search of the immediate area.

'The mechanised company then moved to another area and almost at once was engaged by heavy small-arms fire from isolated groups of the enemy. As the carriers moved, enemy hiding in the reeds were crushed in place. In many cases, dismounted friendly troops actually stepped on the heads of Viet Cong hiding in holes. The sights were almost indescribable. Once, while we were moving rapidly to the left rear of two other tracks, a lone enemy sprang, unarmed, out of the reeds. The gunner opened fire on him at point-blank range with the .50cal. machine gun. Water spray from the bullet strike completely covered the frightened and falling guerilla. Instantly, the track driver turned the vehicle in an obvious effort to run over the man. We passed over him and looked to the rear. Surprisingly enough, a head appeared and a most terrified and shaking young guerilla arose from the water. He appeared to be badly torn up and was bleeding profusely. It was soon discovered that 12 big black leeches were the cause of all of his bleeding. The leeches were removed with the aid of several cigarettes. This guerilla had been hiding in a hole for several hours and the leeches had taken advantage of his immobility. Miraculously, he had escaped the machine gun fire, and had gone

An M41A3 of the 5th Armd. Cav. Regt. supports ARVN infantry as they quell dissenters in the city of Da Nang during the Buddhist Revolt in the spring of 1966. (Tim Page)

between the tracks instead of under them when the driver attempted to crush him.

'Mid-afternoon came before we stopped to take a deep breath and count up the day's tally of Viet Cong. Over 150 Viet Cong had been killed and 38 captured, together with 27 weapons, including one US .50cal. machine gun and two Browning automatic rifles.'

This mechanised operation was a success despite difficult terrain. It clearly showed that, with thorough reconnaissance, successful mechanised operations could be conducted in the difficult terrain of the Delta region in South Vietnam. The Vietnamese who witnessed the green-camouflaged tracked vehicles moving rapidly over the water-soaked fields with fire and smoke belching from the machine guns called the tracks the 'Green Dragons', and were much impressed (see Vanguard 34, *The M113 Series*, Plate A1).

Wounded soldiers are evacuated from an M113 APC bogged in a rice paddy during an operation by the ARVN 9th Div. near Soc Trang, August 1967. (*Armor* Magazine)

Following the success of mechanised operations in the Mekong Delta, further M113 units were formed as Mechanised Rifle Squadrons incorporated into the four armoured cavalry regiments that served one in each of the four Military Regions of South Vietnam. During 1965 the antiquated M24 Chaffees were replaced by M41A3 light tanks, and by the end of the year the eight ARVN Armoured Cavalry Regts. disposed of five tank squadrons (M41A3), 21 mechanised rifle squadrons (M113), three armoured car squadrons (M8) and an experimental self-propelled 4.2 in. mortar troop (M106) with 2nd ACR. Meanwhile the M113s were fitted with gunshields, hatch armour and side-mounted machine guns for greater firepower and protection in their new rôle as fighting vehicles.

The rapid expansion of ARVN armoured units

caused some consternation among the political establishment in Saigon, which knew from bitter experience that it only remained in power at the sufferance of the Armour Command. In early 1966, Prime Minister Ky berated the Chief of Armour, Lt.Col. Tung Bui Luong, about the legitimacy of an unusually high troop strength at the Armour School at Thu Duc (just outside Saigon). Tung explained that this resulted from the approved plan to activate and train new units, and then went on:

'Look, we both know I can overthrow you at will, and you'll simply have to trust me. I'll give you my promise that if I ever do decide to overthrow you I'll give you a day's warning so you can escape. If that's not good enough, get yourself a new Chief of Armour.'

Tung was not replaced; and indeed, in the next months, ARVN armour units saved the Ky government during the so-called 'Buddhist Mutiny' (see Plate C1). The Armour Command was a solid base of political stability thereafter. Two more regiments, the 9th and 10th, became operational in 1966; and in the following year a troop of V100 Commando armoured cars was introduced into each regiment to replace the venerable M8. Ultimately there were 19 Armoured Cavalry Regts., three Tank Regts., (the 20th to 22nd with M48A3 Pattons), and four Armour Bde. Headquarters.

In the VC/NVA Tet Offensive of 1968, the ten ARVN Armoured Cavalry Regiments rode towards the sound of the guns to take a significant part in inflicting a severe military defeat on the enemy fighting in virtually every major town and city in the country. ARVN armour again led the way during Operation 'Lam Son 719' to cut the Ho Chi Minh Trail in Laos in March 1971, when five

Mounting an AN-VSS-1 searchlight above the 90 mm main armament, an M48A3 of 3rd Tank Bn. USMC transports 'grunts' of E/2/3 Marines during 1966. (USMC)

An M67A2 of 1st Tank Bn. USMC sprays a target with flame during an operation in 1968; flame tanks were often incorporated into the standard tank platoons to augment their strength. (USMC)

M41A3 tanks of 1st Sqn., 11th ARVN Cavalry encountered enemy PT-76 and T-54 tanks near Hill 31. In the first major tank-vs.-tank action of the war, the M41s destroyed seven T-54s and 16 PT-76s while losing four of their tanks to RPGs and mines.

The next major tank engagement took place on Easter Sunday 1972 along the Cua Viet River near Dong Ha. The M48A3s of 20th Tank Regt. intercepted a column of PT-76 and T-54 tanks moving south on Highway 1, scattering panicky infantry and heading for the intact Class 60 bridge at Dong Ha. Bringing their 90 mm guns to bear at ranges from 2,800 to 3,200 metres, the M48A3s destroyed 11 tanks before the others turned tail and withdrew. This crucial action allowed ARVN units to establish the 'Dong Ha Line', which delayed the capture of Quang Tri for a month and prevented the fall of I Corps.

Thereafter, tank-vs.-tank actions became commonplace as the NVA resorted to conventional warfare throughout the country. Large numbers of T-54s were committed, not only in I Corps but also in the attacks on Kontum in II Corps and on An Loc in III Corps. With no remaining US ground units, the full brunt of these attacks was countered by ARVN armoured units, with the considerable assistance of US airpower. In 1975 the latter was not available, and ARVN armour was severely hampered by a lack of spares, fuel and ammunition. Only in a last-ditch stand at Xuan Loc was it able to prove its effectiveness, when III Armour Bde. fought to the end against overwhelming NVA forces; but by then, all was lost.

Towed by a Caterpillar D7 'dozer, a disabled M48A3 is escorted to safety by other Pattons of 1st Tank Bn. USMC, accompanied by Marines of 1st Recon Bn., September 1967. (USMC)

A mechanised column of ACAVs and Pattons moves out on an operation; the crew members ride on the outside of the vehicles to reduce the effects of mines. (FMC)

US Marine Corps in Vietnam

In support of the first Marine landings at Da Nang on 8 March 1965 were the M48A3 Pattons of 2nd Ptn., Co. B, 3rd Tank Bn. commanded by Lt. Fran Claybaugh. In the following weeks other platoons of the battalion were landed, and by 8 July all of 3rd Tank Bn. was ashore – the first US tank battalion in Vietnam. In addition to the Patton tanks there were M50A1 Ontos anti-tank vehicles and LVTP-5A1 amphibian tractors ('amtracs'): these were the three principal AFVs used by the Marines during the Vietnam War. By the end of 1965, 1st Tank Bn. was also part of III Marine Amphibious Force in I Corps Tactical Zone.

Besides the M48A3, the 1st and 3rd Tank Bns. fielded the M67A2 flamethrower and the M51 Heavy Recovery Vehicle. The primary rôle of the tanks was in direct support of Marine infantry operations. The standard ratio of armour to infantry was five tanks per infantry battalion. These in turn were divided up into two or three tank sections, and on occasions even single tanks, to support the infantry companies. While this rôle was fundamental to Marine doctrine and remained so throughout the war, Marine tanks performed many other missions. The M48A3 proved its versatility on numerous occasions. It led road convoys and reaction forces; it acted as artillery, firing in the indirect rôle or providing 'Harassing and Interdiction' fire; it provided outpost and strongpoint security; bolstered perimeter defences; reinforced communications; retrieved wounded and dead; crushed enemy bunkers and tunnels; towed damaged vehicles and artillery – any task that offered was attempted.

The Ontos was a lightly armoured air-portable tracked vehicle mounting six 106 mm recoilless rifles, and was peculiar to the Marine Corps. Its intended rôle was the destruction of tanks, but with no enemy armour threat the Ontos did not find much employment in Vietnam except for perimeter defence and, in the early years, against hostile field fortifications in support of infantry operations. The 'amtracs' of the 1st and 3rd Amphibian Tractor Bns. acted as general purpose troop and cargo carriers, both on land and during amphibious operations along the coast and inland waterways of Vietnam. The LVTP5-A1 formed the basis of several special purpose variants including command, engineer, recovery and close-support howitzer models.

Throughout the war, the principal rôle of Marine AFVs was the direct support of dismounted infantry, and they were rarely employed other than under operational control of infantry and in small numbers. Despite these limitations they proved effective according to the dictates of Marine doctrine. The following account by a former commander of a Marine tank company provides an insight into the employment of Marine armour in Vietnam:

'As the days and months wore on in Vietnam, we as Marines found ourselves spread out thinner and thinner over the real estate that we operated in – moving away from the coastal enclaves set up early on in the 1965 time-frame. We now had Marine units operating far inland with fire support bases and logistical areas all over the countryside. Operating with 1st Marine Division in southern I Corps Tactical Zone, the 1st Tank Bn. had three gun companies spread pretty thin providing direct fire support to our infantry. My company – Bravo Co., 1st Tank Bn. – provided direct support for the 5th Marine Regt. headquartered in An Hoa: a real hell hole – "little Dien Bien Phu" as the Marines called it since it sat in a bowl and the NVA constantly fired 122 mm and mortar rounds into the fire base and airstrip. I also supported the 7th Marine Regt. who operated to the north of "Dodge City" and the surrounding areas.

'So providing tank support to six battalions with 17 gun tanks and 4 flame tanks required a bit of a juggling act, to say the least. On a daily basis I would plan, co-ordinate and effect the deployment of these limited assets as best I could. On any given day I would leave my CP (Command Post) at 0900 hrs, as soon as the roads were swept of mines by the engineers, and visit my platoons and various battalion CPs. One day my driver, L/Cpl. Reggie Thompson, and I travelled by jeep to Da Nang, down to Hill 10, Hill 65 and stopped at Hill 37: all this covered about 40 miles of countryside – a lot of Indian country, with no "friendlies" in the area. While at Hill 37 I got a call on the wireless that I had a staff officer visiting my CP at Hill 55 from the tank battalion HQ and that he wanted to see me ASAP. So I saddled up; told Lt. Stone, the tank platoon commander, to give me two tanks for escort through Dodge City; and took off down the road heading for home.

'Now a strange thing happened after we left the last village. An old papa-san looked at us and

A Scorpion 90 mm SPAT (Self-Propelled Anti-Tank Gun) of Co. D, 16th Armor of 173rd Airborne Bde., the only unit to use this vehicle in Vietnam, takes part in an operation in Long Khanh Province during 1966. (US Army)

scurried into his thatched hut. It struck me as a strange manner in which he acted, but we continued down the road. The rice paddies were empty with not a farmer in sight – in fact, not a bird – nothing, just still and quiet. Usually there was animal and human activity in the countryside. I made a radio check with my tanks and proceeded down the road (which by the way, was called "Liberty Road" by Marines). I told my driver that I didn't like the scene; we lit a smoke, and pressed on with our weapons off safe. As we negotiated a blown culvert all hell broke loose: a 15 lb box mine was command-detonated, picking up our jeep and hurling it about six feet in the air. The windscreen was shattered, and the radio blown off its mount in the rear.

'I looked over to see how Thompson was doing, and blood was pouring down his face. We weren't moving, and when the dust settled I said to him, "Let's get the hell out of here!" He said we were stuck; the engine was running at high revs but we weren't moving. I told him to release the clutch – and we leaped out of the ditch. At that moment the little brown bastards opened up with AK-47 fire and the rounds struck the jeep and whipped through the canvas. I returned fire at the ambush team, which was about 100 metres from the road. Shortly afterwards my escort B-13 [M48A3 Patton], commanded by L/Cpl. Flora, called frantically on the wireless, "Bravo Six, Bravo Six, come in, over." I answered, "Bravo Six, go", and he asked me if we were OK. I replied "Affirmative", and proceeded to give a position on the little bastards who had sprung the ambush on us. On Hill 37 S/Sgt. Johnson, the tank platoon sergeant, heard of the ambush over the radio and came tearing down the road. He arrived on the scene and took charge at once, telling L/Cpl. Flora: "Cover me, I'm going in after them."

'As I got out of the kill zone I watched S/Sgt. Johnson maneuver in a cat-and-mouse style, stalking the NVA killer team. Firing his sky-mounted .50cal. MG into the thicket, he moved toward the NVA position. They didn't return fire, but suddenly broke and ran. S/Sgt. Johnson fired over their heads and they hit the deck, then got up and ran again. At point blank range, he opened fire with a 90 mm HE round and blew them away. Result: five NVA wasted . . . I was on my way to my CP, glad that was behind me, when a sniper opened up – so I returned fire and blew him away. I drove back to my tank company HQ. It was just another day in the Corps in Nam.'

ACAVs and troops of 2nd Bn., 47th Inf. (Mech.) of 9th Inf. Div. advance through close terrain during a 'search and destroy' operation. (US Army)

US Army Armour in Vietnam

To most Army officers at the Military Assistance Command Vietnam (MACV), ensconced in their air-conditioned bunkers in the 'Pentagon East' outside Saigon, the war against the Viet Cong was suited only to infantry; even Special Forces units were viewed with suspicion. To them, the solution to the military problem was more men and more helicopters. It was believed that armour units, in particular, could play no significant part in Vietnam because of the terrain, the enemy and the nature of area warfare – when fighting is likely to occur from any direction at any time. This attitude was compounded by political considerations which limited available manpower and logistical support.

As a result, the first US Army divisions deployed to Vietnam in 1965 were stripped of their tank battalions, and their mechanised infantry battalions were dismounted. However, the nature of the war and the enemy were changing, from small guerilla units to well trained and equipped North Vietnamese Army (NVA) regiments and divisions. While retaining many facets of guerilla warfare, these forces adopted conventional tactics whenever the need arose; their armament expanded to include modern automatic small arms, heavier mortars and artillery, an effective anti-vehicle and anti-aircraft capability, as well as considerable expertise in the widespread use of mines. Armoured fighting vehicles, with their inherent protection against small arms and anti-personnel mines, and with the mobility and firepower to gain a tactical advantage, became a necessity even in the hidebound minds of MACV.

In 1966 the 11th Armored Cavalry Regt., and the 25th Infantry Division complete with its armoured units – the 3rd Sqn., 4th Cavalry; the 1st Bn., 5th Infantry (Mechanized); and 1st Bn., 69th Armor – arrived in Vietnam. These few mounted formations achieved significant success in combat during that year and into 1967. The 11th Armd. Cav. – 'The Blackhorse Regiment' – proved that mounted units could conduct operations more effectively than dismounted ones in enemy-dominated areas such as the 'Iron Triangle' and War Zone C, north-west of Saigon. The large multi-unit operations 'Cedar Falls' and 'Junction City' I and II, in the spring of 1967, dispelled all doubts about the effectiveness of armour in Vietnam.

At the same time, a major study of armour operations (*Mechanized and Armor Combat Operations in Vietnam*) concluded that while the type of warfare waged in Vietnam was markedly different from the more conventional campaigns of the Second World War and Korea, armour doctrine remained valid; and by modifying tactics and techniques to meet the requirements of area warfare, as well as weather and terrain in certain parts of the country, armoured units could be effectively employed in most areas and for a variety of missions.

In consequence, more armoured formations were deployed to Vietnam, where they played an increasingly significant and vital rôle, eventually contributing more than half of the Army's total combat power. On offensive operations they conducted 'search and destroy' missions, which involved area reconnaissance with the intention of engaging the enemy wherever he was to be found and destroying him by the generation of sufficient combat power by the unit and supporting arms. In area warfare, security missions protecting convoys, roads and bases are a high priority and armoured/mechanised units are well suited to these; and particularly to the reaction force rôle when the swift reinforcement of units in contact is necessary. At the outset, doctrine for mechanised infantry emphasised the armoured personnel carrier (APC) as a means of transporting infantry to battle. In Vietnam most mechanised units used the M113 APC as a vehicle from which the infantry fought, and to this end the M113 was equipped with a variety of machine guns and armour shields for greater firepower and protection. In this guise it became known as the Armored Cavalry Assault Vehicle or ACAV, and was the most important AFV of the war.

Of all the armour formations employed in Vietnam, the most effective were the divisional armoured cavalry squadrons and those of the 11th Armd. Cav. Regt.: they were used more frequently as combat manoeuvre battalions than in their traditional reconnaissance rôle. Armoured cavalry was an excellent force when rapid reaction, swift movement, high firepower and aggressive pursuit were required. Its ready-made combined arms team organisation was highly suited to meet the many contingencies of area warfare, as the

Shaded beneath a sunshield, the commander of an M48A3 of Tp. C, 3rd Sqn., 5th Cav. of 9th Inf. Div. stands perimeter guard during Operation 'Junction City' near Quan Loi, March 1967. (US Army)

following battle account vividly confirms.

The battle of Binh An was fought by the 3rd Sqn., 5th Cavalry of 9th Infantry Division, reinforced by three companies of the 1st Air Cavalry Division, and took place on 27 and 28 June 1968 on the sandy beaches in the northern part of I Corps Tactical Zone. The '3rd of the 5th' Cav. had been operating in the area for about two months; the squadron had been detached from the 9th Division after the 1968 Tet Offensive had begun and had worked in turn for the 1st Marine Division at Da Nang, the 3rd Marine Division at Dong Ha, the 101st Airborne at Phu Bai, and finally for the 1st Air Cavalry Division in the area of operations (AO) where this battle took place.

Under the operational control of the 2nd Bde., 1st Air Cav. Div., the squadron had been assigned the missions of securing the Wunder Beach complex and the access road leading to Highway 1, and of reconnaissance operations throughout the entire AO. The squadron was reinforced by two infantry companies under operational control on a rotating basis. Generally, Wunder Beach was held with one infantry company, the squadron headquarters troop and a guard detail drawn from all tenant units in the complex. The second infantry company was stationed on the access road at Fire Support Base (FSB) Hardcore. One cavalry troop was always conducting operations nearby, able to provide a rapid reaction force if needed. The two other cavalry troops conducted continuous reconnaissance operations throughout the AO.

The AO measured about 35 km along the beach and 12 km inland at its widest point. Four kilometres of the width was beach dotted with occasional patches of bamboo which sheltered civilian homes, most of which were abandoned. The rest of the AO was dry rice paddy. NVA forces were active in the area and a major NVA supply route ran through it. There was an abundance of food, so

The Armored Cavalry Assault Vehicle or ACAV was the most numerous and important AFV of the Vietnam War. This ACAV BALL LOVE belongs to Tp. B, 1st Sqn., 11th Armd. Cav. Regt. (Geoff Cornish)

M48A3 Pattons of Tp. C, 3rd Sqn., 4th Cav. of 25th Inf. Div. support the division's 1st Bn., 35th Inf. during a 'search and destroy' operation, June 1967. (US Army)

large NVA units were accustomed to moving into the villages and quartering their troops with the local civilians for several days before moving on.

On the morning of 27 June the squadron was dispersed throughout the AO. Troop A had completed a night operation and had returned to the beach complex to rest and maintain their vehicles, having left one platoon at FSB Hardcore. Troop B, with three engineer bulldozers attached, was engaged in a search of 'The Street without Joy' bordering Highway 1. The AO had been temporarily extended northwards, and Troop C, together with Troop D, 1st Sqn., 9th Cav. (Air), was performing an 'economy of force' mission in support of US Marine operations to the north. Troop D, 1/9th Cav. was the dismounted ground troop of the air cavalry squadron of the 1st Air Cav. Div., and had been attached to the squadron in addition to the two above-mentioned infantry companies. At this time the two units were returning to Wunder Beach, conducting what was planned to be a two-day reconnaissance in force along the way.

At 0900 hrs Troop C and Troop D received RPG and small arms fire as they approached the fringes of the village of Binh An. The fire was returned. Troop C commander immediately sent a portion of his troop in a flanking manoeuvre to the west; minutes later, one of the leading tanks was hit by an RPG south-west of the village. Considering the distance between the point where the initial contact was made and the point where the tank was hit, Lt.Col. Hugh J. Bartley, the squadron commander, deduced that a large unit was occupying the village.

At 0923 hrs he ordered Troop A to move from Wunder Beach to the site of the contact. Concurrently, the second group of NVA withdrew into the village, and the lead elements of Troop C proceeded to the coast where the entire population of Binh An, about 400 people in all, was found to be evacuating the village. With this information to hand, Lt.Col. Bartley ordered Troop B to move from 'The Street without Joy' to the contact. At the same time Troop C was ordered to detain the fleeing civilians. An NVA soldier was discovered in their midst and captured alive. When interrogated, he said that the 300-man K14 Bn. of the 812th NVA Regt. was emplaced in the village.

With two troops in contact and two more on the way, the battle began to take shape. As Troop B came in on the north and Troop A closed in to the south, Troop C contracted its lines to take over the middle portion of the cordon, carrying Troop D, 1/9th Cav. with it. By 1030 hrs the stage was set, with four cavalry troops in position around Binh An. During daylight hours there could be no escape from the village due to the superior visibility and fields of fire commanded by the squadron. Therefore, the task which remained was to reduce the position.

The next seven hours were spent in pounding the enemy. In addition to helicopter gunship aerial rocket artillery and Marine artillery, which had been made available on initial contact, the squadron soon had TAC air from Da Nang, Marine artillery firing from Quang Tri, and the destroyers *O'Brien* and *Edson* with 5 in. guns standing offshore. Each element of fire support had its own controller, and each integrated its fire with the plan conceived by the squadron commander and the fire support co-ordination center (FSCC). The area inside the cordon erupted as hundreds of shells crashed in on the target. A naval observer reported the shelling to be so fierce that NVA soldiers were diving into the sea to escape its effect.

To add strength to the cordon, two infantry companies were heli-lifted in during the afternoon: Co. C, 1st Bn., 5th Cav. came into a Landing Zone (LZ) adjacent to Troop B to the north, while Co. C, 2nd Bn., 5th Cav. landed in an LZ adjacent to Troop A and joined it. (Interestingly, the only unit involved in the ground fighting that day which was not a former part of the old 5th Cav. Regt. was Troop D of the 9th Cavalry. It was literally a 5th Cavalry field day.)

Because of its superior mobility and preponderance of firepower the squadron had a distinct advantage over the enemy, since the travel time for a 'track' (AFV) around the outside of the Binh An cordon was much shorter than for an NVA foot soldier moving from the centre of the village through the heavy sand to the perimeter. The tanks and APCs could reinforce any part of the cordon as quickly as an attack of breakout proportions could be mounted. There was little danger, therefore, of a mass breakout by the entire enemy battalion.

As the afternoon passed, it became clear that the battle could not be concluded that day. Furthermore, a large number of the trapped battalion were likely to escape under the cover of darkness unless their command structure was destroyed by nightfall. Thus it was decided to try to overrun the position before dark and destroy the enemy's capability for effective operations during the night, while the main phase of the mopping-up operations was to be left until the next day.

Troop C was selected for the assault because it would be attacking towards the sea. The enemy position was assaulted with the entire troop on line. However, the attack was quickly stalled by a drainage ditch covered by RPG and small arms fire.

An ACAV of 1st Sqn., 1st Cav. retrieves a stranded companion during a sweep of the 'Rice Bowl' near Duc Pho, August 1969; the ACAV is armed with a .50cal. Browning and two 7.62 mm M60 machine guns. (US Army)

Troop C was ordered to hold, and the attack mission was passed to Troop B, which attacked the flank of the main bunker system during the last hour of daylight. With its attached infantry dispersed between the tracked vehicles, Troop B moved out on line to attack the village from the north. To allow it to use all its weapons to the front, the soldiers of Troop A on the south side of the cordon sheltered inside their armoured vehicles. Troop B swept through the encircled battalion until its fire began to ricochet off the Troop A vehicles; it then turned around to plough through the enemy once more, wreaking havoc in its path. As darkness fell, Troop B resumed its blocking positions in the cordon.

The unmerciful pounding of the North Vietnamese Army's K14 Bn. continued throughout the night. Overhead a USAF C-47 was on station all night, dropping flares to provide sufficient light for observers to adjust artillery and naval gunfire and to control tactical air strikes. The cruiser USS *Boston* arrived offshore just after dark, and expended her basic load of 8 in. shells upon the enemy. Most of the air strikes carried napalm and, overall, the disputed ground resembled the mouth of hell. No mass break-out by the enemy was attempted, and only small groups or individuals tried to escape by sea. M48A3 tanks with searchlights illuminated the beaches, exposing the fugitives, and those who made it beyond the surf were despatched by two US Navy Swift boats patrolling close inshore. Others who tried to slip through the landward cordon were detected by night vision devices and killed or driven back by small arms fire.

Morning brought an increase in the bombardment until a 'psyops' (psychological operations) team flew over Binh An, urging the NVA to surrender. No response was noted within the allotted time, and Troop B began the final assault at 0930 hrs meeting only scattered resistance. It was eliminated without friendly casualties. For the next two days 3/5th Cavalry searched the battle area with the assistance of engineer bulldozers. It became apparent that K14 Bn. had been virtually annihilated: 277 NVA soldiers were killed or captured including the battalion CO, his staff and all the company commanders. Only three American soldiers were killed during the battle.

The executive officer of the 3/5th Cav., Maj. Michael D. Mahler, wrote of the battle several years later: 'We had once more stumbled into a situation and had been able to turn it to our advantage. But it was more than stumbling, and it was not luck that brought success. It was soldiers in hot steel vehicles out in the glaring sand looking and poking until the enemy, North Vietnamese and Viet Cong, never knew when or where an armored column would crop up next.' One battle-seasoned NVA sergeant who had evidently been part of the force that first fired on Troop C put it differently while being questioned at the brigade interrogation point. He was still in shock, sitting cross-legged on the ground, fists clenched and eyes closed in frustration and defeat, as he said over and over again: 'I *told* them not to shoot at those tanks! I *told* them not to shoot at those tanks . . . !'

An M48A3 gunner of 1st Sqn., 4th Cav., 1st Inf. Div. engages a target with main armament rounds during an operation in 1969. (Geoff Cornish)

* * *

While the M48A3 Patton, the ACAV and the M113 family were the principal AFVs of the Vietnam War, there were a host of others whose contributions in terms of mobility and firepower were significant: none more so than the M42A1 'Dusters' and M55 Quad 50s of the Air Defense Artillery (ADA) battalions. Prior to its involvement in Vietnam the US Army had considered antiaircraft guns obsolete and had equipped itself with missile systems, relegating its self-propelled guns to the Reserve and National Guard. These had to be retrieved in order to equip the three automatic weapon battalions that served in Vietnam from

1966. Each battalion had a headquarters, four Duster batteries, an attached M55 machine gun battery and an attached searchlight battery. With a personnel strength of approximately 1,000 men, it was one of the larger type of battalions in Vietnam. The Duster batteries had a headquarters and two firing platoons; the machine gun battery, an HQ and six machine gun sections.

The 1st Bn. (Automatic Weapon Self-Propelled), 44th Artillery was the first ADA battalion to arrive in Vietnam in November 1966. 1/44th Artillery was to become one of the most decorated of artillery units, supporting the Marines in Hue and at Khe Sanh as well as Army divisions in the rugged I Corps region. The battalion was assigned to I Field Force Vietnam Artillery and was located at Dong Ha. It served in Vietnam until December 1971.

The 4th Bn. (AWSP), 60th Artillery arrived in Vietnam in March 1967 and became part of 41st Artillery Group of I Field Force Vietnam (1FFV) at Qui Nhon in II CTZ. In February 1968 it was attached to 1FFV Artillery and moved to An Khe in June, and then to Tuy Hoa from late 1970 up to its departure from Vietnam in December 1971.

The 5th Bn. (AWSP), 2nd Artillery arrived in Vietnam in November 1966 and was stationed at Long Binh as part of 11FFV Artillery – see Plate F1. The battalion left Vietnam in June 1971.

Mounted on an M41 light tank chassis, the twin 40 mm Bofors fully automatic guns gave the Duster a combination of devastating firepower and mobility. With no enemy aircraft to counter, the Dusters and Quad 50s were used in the ground support rôle, adding their impressive firepower to the tremendous volume of fire expended by American units in Vietnam. In their five years of war service, the automatic weapon battalions fired over four million rounds of 40 mm ammunition and over ten million rounds of Quad 50 ammunition. The 40 mm HEIT (High Explosive Incendiary Tracer) projectile weighed approximately 2 lbs, with a muzzle velocity of 2,870 feet per second. The effect of the HEIT round against personnel in the open or inside hasty fortifications was appalling.

The Duster also delivered effective indirect fire, both for 'Harassing and Interdiction' and in the counter-battery rôle. Enemy units learned to set up mortar, recoilless rifle and rocket positions just beyond the maximum range of the Duster's regular 40 mm self-destruct ammunition. The NVA tried this tactic during the siege of Ben Het in March 1969, when PT-76 amphibious tanks of 202nd Armd. Regt. attempted to overrun the Special Forces camp. The two Duster crews of 1/44th Artillery responded by loading one gun with regular ammunition and the other with long-range ammunition. Upon observing the mortar, recoilless rifles and rocket flashes, the crews made their direct-fire adjustments with regular ammunition and then switched to the long-range variety to silence the enemy positions.

The Dusters and M55s were never available in sufficient numbers, and they were normally parcelled out to mechanised infantry or armoured cavalry units scattered the length and breadth of Vietnam. They provided convoy escort on the 'Street without Joy'; 'circled the wagons' with infantry in hostile places like the Ia Drang Valley; floated down the Mekong River on barges; defended fire support bases against ground attack; and conducted reconnaissance by fire for infantry heading into enemy sanctuaries such as the Michelin Rubber Plantation.

Convoy escort duty was hazardous and nerve-racking. Normally, the lead vehicle – 'the front door' – covered the left side of the road while the rear vehicle covered the right side. If caught in an ambush, Dusters pulled off the road, traversed their guns, and provided covering fire for the convoy's other vehicles as they hurried to escape the kill zone. The tactic was effective, but it meant that Duster crews spent what seemed like an eternity in the kill zone. SFC Steve Nash recounts:

'I did three tours in Vietnam. I did the first two with the 5/2nd Artillery in '68 and '69, and the last one with the 1/44th Artillery in '70 and '71. My first track was called "Triple Deuce", because we were the second track in the second squad of the second platoon. I started out as assistant gunner and worked my way up to track commander and squad leader. I spent the second tour on a track called "The Dirty Five" – there were four of us, and the track made five. I spent the third tour with the 1st of the 44th up in I Corps on a track called "Pa Kettle". We were the "front door" on convoy duty and "Ma Kettle" was the "back door".

'I was wounded twice. The second time was worse. I was on "Pa Kettle" when it happened. We

IC-94113

1: M24 Chaffee, 1er Régt. de Chasseurs à Cheval; Tonkin, 1953

2: M29C Crabe, 1er Régt. Étranger de Cavalerie; Cochinchina, 1951

A

1: M24 Chaffee, Esc. de M. du 1er RCC; Dien Bien Phu, 1954

2: M5A1, 5eRégt. de Cuirassiers, GM 100; Annam, 1954

1: M41A3, 5th Armd.Cav. Regt., ARVN; Da Nang, 1966

2: M50A1 Ontos, 3rd A/T Bn., USMC; I CTZ, 1967

1: M48A3, A Co.HQ, 1st Tank Bn.,USMC; Hue, 1968

2: ACAV, D Co., 1st Sqn., 11th Armd.Cav.; III CTZ, 1969

D

1: M35A2, 444th Trspt.Co.; Qui Nhon, II CTZ, 1968

2: M577A1, HQ 2nd Sqn., 11th Armd.Cav.; Bien Hoa, 1969

E

1: M42A1 Duster, Bty.D, 5th AWSP Bn., 2nd Arty.; Quan Loi, 1969

2: M109 155 mm SP, Bty.L, 4th Bn., 12th Marines; I CTZ, 1967

F

1: M551 Sheridan, Tp.B, 1st Sqn., 11th Armd.Cav.; An Loc, 1969

2: M728 CEV, 919th Eng.Co., 11th Armd.Cav.; Quan Loi, 1969

1: Centurion Mk.5/1 (Aust.), A Sqn., 1st Armd.Regt., 1st ATF; Phuoc Tuy, 1970

2: T-59, 203rd Armd.Regt., NVA; Saigon, 30 April 1975

H

were pulling convoy duty not far from Firebase Tennessee near Dau Tieng, and had to leave the second track behind because of a blown engine. We made a looping left turn when Charlie hit us with B-22 and B-40 rockets. An RPG came through the ready rack and exploded inside the tub. The explosion knocked the track off the road into a rice paddy. My assistant gunner lived just long enough to scream my name. I got hit by shrapnel in the abdomen. We got the track back on the road and were headed for LZ Bird, a nearby firebase, when we saw a Huey. We popped smoke grenades, and the Huey came down and picked up the wounded. I was taken to the 24th Evac and ended up in Japan.'

Most Dusters towed a trailer that served the crew as a baggage car for personal belongings. The normal combat load also included culvert halves, chain-link fencing and empty sandbags. When the Duster pulled into a night defensive position (NDP), the crew erected the culvert halves near the vehicle. Once the crews had covered them with two or three layers of sandbags and had constructed a blast wall, the culvert halves became bunkers that provided effective protection from mortars. The chain-link fencing, when staked out in front of the vehicle, stopped RPGs (Rocket Propelled Grenades).

A fire base was fortunate if it had air defence vehicles on its perimeter. A typical enemy attack against an isolated fire base or NDP began with a mortar barrage designed to drive the defenders into their bunkers. Then specially-trained sappers – incredibly brave men, who stripped to loincloths and slung satchel charges around their bodies – snaked through the densest concertina wire and around the defensive Claymore mines, while the enemy gunners switched from mortars to RPGs, hoping the defenders would fail to distinguish between them and would remain in their bunkers. Having cleared the wire, the sappers would dash through the position hurling satchel charges into bunkers and vehicles, trying to cause maximum casualties and material damage. If they caused sufficient havoc, the enemy commander might follow up their success by launching a full-scale infantry assault. Being overrun became the ultimate Vietnam nightmare.

Shooting at minimal elevations, both the Duster and Quad 50 generated devastating ground fires; their crews called it 'mowing grass'. The volume of fire during 'mad minutes', when all weapons on the perimeter fired simultaneously for a set time, was often so intimidating that it prevented ground attacks from being launched. When VC/NVA attacks were pressed home, the Duster was often a prime target. Knowing that the enemy would attempt to silence Dusters at the beginning of an attack, units moved their vehicles from one alternate firing position to another after dark in order to conceal their location.

An M48A3 'dozer tank of the 919th Eng. Co., 11ACR, waits while the road ahead is swept for mines – the bane of AFVs in Vietnam and the cause of almost 75 per cent of combat vehicle casualties. (US Army)

The Dusters spent most daylight hours on road security or convoy escort duty. They spent the nights on base camp or fire base perimeters, or simply 'circled the wagons' with the unit they were supporting. Automatic weapon crews listened to the Armed Forces Network Vietnam on their transistor radios, which played wholesome numbers like *The Green, Green Grass of Home* and *We've Got to Get Out of This Place*, an early 1960s' rock 'n' roll hit whose popularity lasted the length of the war, for obvious reasons. They carried cassette players into battle and would sometimes turn the volume up full blast during fire-fights. A Jimi Hendrix album was preferred background music for a fire-fight. It was something that came naturally after watching Hollywood war movies: the need for a soundtrack!

With its high silhouette, open turret and bulky configuration, the Duster was an imposing vehicle but to the infantry and cavalry it was simply a valuable anti-personnel weapon – though one which naturally attracted more than its share of enemy attention. It was a fairly 'rare beast', and the troops' reactions were probably typified by three mud-spattered airborne troopers who encountered a Duster at Phan Rang in 1967. The three troopers had come down out of the mountains just before the monsoon at the end of their one-year tour and had been ordered on perimeter guard for their last night in the base camp. They belonged to the 101st Airborne (Airmobile) Div. and knew next to nothing about tracks, having spent their entire tour miles from the nearest road. They had never seen a Duster until they came onto the perimeter in the gathering twilight.

'What is it?' asked one of the troopers.

'It's a Duster, an M42,' the track commander answered.

'You guys armoured cav?'

'Naw. We're ADA.'

'AD what?'

'Air Defense Artillery.'

The three troopers mulled that over for a while.

'Looks like it can really rock 'n' roll,' said one.

'Want to see it mow some grass?' the gunner asked.

'Sure.'

The gunner and track commander climbed into the turret and fired four long bursts beyond the concertina wire.

'Psychedelic!' one of the troopers exclaimed.

'Airborne!' said another.

'Bet it draws a lot of fire,' the third one said.

'No lie, GI,' the track commander answered.

First deployed in early 1969, the M551 Sheridan suffered a rash of reliability problems, and was vulnerable to mine damage which was ameliorated by the addition of 'belly armour' visible on the lower hull front and under the sponsons of this Sheridan BRANDED of Tp. B, 1/11 ACR. (Geoff Cornish)

'Mowing grass' – an M42A1 Duster of 5th Bn., 2nd Arty. 'turns on the rock 'n' roll' as it engages a target in III CTZ. (US Army)

The three troopers picked up their packs and moved on past the fighting positions close to the Duster, which no 'short-timer' wished to occupy, to others farther along the perimeter.

North Vietnamese Armour in Vietnam

Until the final years of the war the North Vietnamese Army made little use of its armoured force, which had been created in 1959. Prior to the conventional invasion of 1972, the only notable and successful attack by NVA armour was against the Lang Vei Special Forces Camp near Khe Sanh on 6–7 February 1968. The camp was held by a Special Forces 'A' Team of 24 'Green Berets' and four under-strength Civilian Irregular Defense Group (CIDG) companies of Bru Montagnards, with a detachment of Vietnamese Special Forces. In all, over 480 soldiers manned the emplacements at Lang Vei which housed two 106 mm and four 57 mm recoilless rifles, two 4.2 in. and six 81 mm mortars, as well as crates of M-72 light anti-tank weapons (LAWs) placed around the camp.

To support the position, Marine artillery at Khe Sanh Combat Base, just eight kilometres to the east, was on call around the clock, using the call-sign 'Intrigue'. Also on call were AC-47 'Spooky' gunships in case of night attack, and F-4 Phantoms and Huey helicopter gunships for close support. Numerous Claymore mines and trip flares ringed the perimeter and its concertina wire but no anti-tank mines were laid due to an MACV directive which dismissed the possibility of tank attack.

At 2230 hrs on 6 February 1968, a grenade exploded and a trip flare bathed the perimeter in light. In its whitish glow, NVA assault troops breached the wire with satchel charges and within minutes were fighting the Montagnards in the forward trenches. Meanwhile, a 'Green Beret' in the observation tower atop the Tactical Operations Center spotted two PT-76 amphibious tanks, whose commanders were directing sappers probing for anti-tank mines. Grabbing the field telephone, he called, 'We got tanks in the wire!', and then scrambled down the ladder to inform the camp commander, Capt. Frank Willoughby. Another 'Green Beret', Sgt. John Early, saw five PT-76s rumbling towards his position through the smoke and dust, with infantry moving up behind them.

Calling the TOC, Early succinctly summed up the situation: 'Jesus Christ, I've got five tanks and a couple of hundred gooks on top of me. They're all over the f***ing place. Get me some illumination!' Willoughby immediately ordered the camp radio operator, SP4 Frank Dooms, to contact Khe Sanh and Da Nang for fire support.

'Intrigue, Intrigue, this is Brassy Study, over! We are taking a heavy ground attack and have armor in the wire. Stand by for fire mission, over.'

The Marines at Khe Sanh were sceptical about the tanks.

'Brassy, this is Intrigue. Are you sure about that armor?'

'Roger, roger, that is affirm. We have tanks in the perimeter.'

'Can you see them from your location?'

SP4 Dooms at Lang Vei shouted into the handset with frustration: 'Affirmative, affirmative! I can hear the engines backfiring. They're firing into the bunkers!'

The Marine operator still seemed unable to comprehend the situation and after a moment of silence, he replied, 'Negative, Brassy. That must be the sound of your generators backfiring.'

Before Dooms could answer an HE shell blasted in the TOC door, showering him with dirt and debris. Calmly retrieving the handset from the floor, he replied: 'Intrigue, be advised: one of our generators just blew down the bunker door!'

Eventually US artillery began to pound the outer edges of the camp, and shortly after 0100 hrs it was joined by air strikes from F-4 Phantoms and A-1 Skyraiders. On the ground the defenders fell back as the tanks destroyed positions and bunkers at point-blank range. A total of 13 PT-76 tanks attacked Lang Vei; a few were stopped by recoilless rifle fire, but when the M-72 LAWs proved to be defective the only way to halt them was to climb on to their hulls, pry open the hatches and drop in hand grenades. Beloved of film directors, this procedure is less popular with combat soldiers . . .

A Duster crew of the '1st of the 44th' feed the dual 40 mm Bofors during a fire mission in support of Marine operations near the Khe Sanh Combat Base in 1967. (USMC)

Two members of the 1st Air Cav. Div. drag a wounded comrade across Highway 1 as a Duster of 1st Bn., 44th Arty., returns fire in an ambush on 22 February 1968, when the division was moving southwards towards Hue City during the Tet Offensive. (*Armor* Magazine)

Long into the next day the camp was bombarded by artillery and air strikes, as the few survivors sheltered in the bunker beneath the TOC. Around 1600 hrs, with low-flying Phantoms screaming overhead on dummy bomb runs to distract the NVA, Willoughby and his men broke out of the camp, and were airlifted to Khe Sanh by helicopter. As the Special Forces soldiers arrived at the Marine combat base many of them were nearly incoherent: some with rage at being sacrificed, some just numb after two days of hand-to-hand combat. The camp was a total loss: of 484 Vietnamese, Bru, Hre and American personnel, almost all were dead or captured. Of the Special Forces 'A' Team, half were dead and two spent five years as PoWs. All the survivors were wounded, some two or three times. For the first time in the Vietnam War tanks had been employed against Allied troops. Lang Vei will also be remembered as the place where more decorations for valour were won by a Special Forces unit than in any other action in the war.

In the Easter offensive of 1972, the NVA used tanks in large numbers to spearhead attacks on three separate fronts. The main thrust across the northern Demilitarised Zone (DMZ) began on 30 March with 100 tanks in the van. Despite the initial success of breaking the 3rd ARVN Div., the tanks were checked by the ARVN 20th Tank Regt., and their subsequent hesitant employment allowed the ARVN enough time to form a stable defence line.

For the attacks on Kontum and Binh Long Provinces the NVA also used tanks, but due to a lack of effective artillery support, combined with an absence of accompanying infantry and their piecemeal employment in small groups, they were easy prey for ARVN anti-armour weapons. Furthermore, once the initial bad weather cleared, USAF and RVN ground-attack planes destroyed many enemy AFVs on all three fronts. By the end of the offensive the NVA had sustained some 60,000 casualties and had lost 250 AFVs.

The first large-scale use of AFVs by the NVA illustrated many of the problems associated with their employment. In a massive re-equipment and reorganisation programme, NVA divisions were trained in combined arms operations with the emphasis on the shock effect and firepower of armour and artillery closely supported by infantry and sapper groups. The effectiveness of the new doctrine was demonstrated in ruthless campaigns to eradicate anti-communist groups in Laos and Cambodia, and subsequently in December 1974 in the attack on Phuoc Long Province when a combined infantry and armour assault on the provincial capital, Phuoc Binh, quickly led to its capture.

Emboldened by this success, the NVA began planning a major strategic offensive against the RVN for the spring of 1975. Having learnt the lessons of 1972, armoured units incorporated a large

An M88 VTR (Vehicle Tracked Recovery) lowers a powerpack into the belly of an M48A3 of 1st Bn., 69th Armor; the M88 was the versatile workhorse of maintenance personnel, but there were never sufficient to support all the far-flung armoured units in Vietnam. (*Armor* **Magazine)**

proportion of air defence weapons (ZSU-57-2 and ZSU-23-4) and were only employed for decisive engagements which would have the greatest influence on the prevailing strategic situation. For this reason AFVs were not used in the diversionary actions of the 'Tay Nguyen Campaign' in the Central Highlands, but were amassed for the major assault on Ban Me Thout.

The NVA identified two specific tactics for the use of armoured forces – the 'sudden assault' and the 'deep advance'. The notion of the sudden assault implied crushing enemy resistance by a quick attack using the shock effect of AFVs to throw the enemy off balance. This technique was used against population centres such as Bien Hoa, Hoc Mon and Xuan Loc. A successful 'sudden assault' opened the way for an effective 'deep advance' or pursuit. By advancing in tight combined arms groups, with infantry in APCs, trucks and captured vehicles, the tanks maintained constant pressure on a withdrawing enemy while at the same time inflicting heavy casualties on ARVN units. When

The M60 Main Battle Tank did not serve in Vietnam, but two of its variants did: the M728 CEV, and the M60 Armored Vehicle Launched Bridge (AVLB) shown here during Operation 'Santa Fe' in November 1967. (US Army)

resistance was encountered the leading units deployed for a 'sudden assault' while following units bypassed the enemy location to continue the 'deep advance'. By these means the NVA armoured units were able to cover an average of 50 kilometres a day; and within two months of the start of the 'Ho Chi Minh Campaign' were in striking distance of the capital of the Republic of Vietnam.

The final order for the attack on Saigon was issued during the night of 29 April by the General Mobile Command of the NVA on the outskirts of Bien Hoa. Four armoured columns were to converge on Saigon at sunrise with the infantry following. As early as the afternoon of 23 April the 203rd Armd. Regt. knew that its mission was to take Saigon, but at that time only two of its tank squadrons had arrived at Suoi Cat, 40 miles east of the capital. The others, after occupying Hue and Da Nang, had barely reached Phan Thiet and Phan Rang on the coast, so the tanks of the advance guard had to wait.

A Soviet-built T-54 bearing the number '843' on the turret sides lay concealed under a covering of

A Civilian Irregular Defense Group (CIDG) soldier chats with the crew of an M55 'Quad 50' of Bty. D, 71st Arty., providing perimeter defence at Fire Support Base 'Mike Smith' in 1970. (US Army)

Artillery units employed a range of self-propelled guns and howitzers during the Vietnam War, although they were seldom used in a mobile rôle; here an M107 175 mm self-propelled gun of 23rd Arty. Gp. blasts away at the enemy near Tay Ninh in 1967. (US Army)

coconut-palm branches as its crew considered the brief order given them by the regiment's political commissar: 'To Doc Lap Palace as soon as possible.' The tank commander was Bui Quang Than, the driver Lu Van Hao, the gunner Thai Ba Minh and the loader Nguyen Van Ky. All were volunteers from far to the north, but their directions were precise: 'Cross the Thi Nghe bridge. Proceed straight ahead on Hong Tap Tu Street. Go seven blocks and turn left. Doc Lap is right in front of you.'

The tanks set out at 0500 hrs in close formation, with Commander Piu and Commissar Tung of the regimental headquarters in the centre of the column. The advance on Saigon was later recounted by one of the participants, Nguyen Trung Tanh:

'Puppet [i.e. ARVN] artillery had been firing at us all night from the Thu Doc Military School, the Police School, and from behind the Ha Thien Cement Factory. Our cannons returned shot for shot while our engineers repaired the bridge in the Buy district, which the retreating puppets had had time to blow up.

'We started at five o'clock. We no longer had anything to fear from the air force, and we kept our anti-aircraft batteries with their sights lowered. By six, Long Binh was already behind us and we had

Known as the 'Duck' from its shape, or simply the 'V' from its designation V-100, the Cadillac-Gage M706 Commando was the principal armoured car used by US forces in Vietnam; its major rôle was convoy escort. (Geoff Cornish)

An M48A3, named IRON CITY and THE MAX, of 2nd Bn., 34th Armor supports troops of the 25th Inf. Div. during an operation in the Michelin Rubber Plantation, September 1970; moments after this photograph was taken a soldier stepped on a mine – death came suddenly in Vietnam. (US Army)

destroyed four of the puppets' M113 armoured vehicles. At the Rach Chiec bridge some enemy tanks held us up a little by firing anti-tank missiles, but our leading squadron destroyed them one by one. At eleven we were on the Thi Nghe bridge.

'The door to Saigon was open in front of us. The first three tanks were already rolling down Hong Tap Tu Street when two enemy M41s blocked our way, firing like mad. Our tank '390' pierced one of them with a shell; the other went up in flames, hit by Bui Quang Than's tank '843'. The street, however, was blocked, and tank '843' turned left and found itself on Mac Dinh Chi Street. It had lost its way. Tank leader Than saw two puppet soldiers in camouflage uniforms on the sidewalk.

'"Where is the Doc Lap Palace?" Than asked. One didn't answer; the other said: "I know."

'Than removed their uniform jackets and had them get on to the tank, which turned right at the next corner. Seeing a girl on a Honda, he stood up straight in the tank and shouted: "How do we get to Doc Lap Palace, please?"

'"You're on Thong Nhat Avenue. There's the palace, right in front of you," she answered.

'Tank '843' rolled on to Doc Lap. It was noon.'

After crashing through the gates of the presidential palace and slewing to a halt on the grass of the immaculate lawn, Than, with an AK-47 in one hand and an NLF flag pulled from the radio antenna in the other, jumped from the turret and ran up the palace steps. Moments later Than was on the roof unfurling the flag from the highest pole above the palace. The time was 1215 hrs: and Saigon had fallen.

The Plates

A1: METZ, M24 Chaffee of 2e Peloton, 2e Escadron, 1er Régiment de Chasseurs à Cheval; Operation 'Mouette', Tonkin, November 1953

With the distinctive regimental insignia on the turret sides, M24 METZ takes part in an operation against the Viet Minh 304th Div. near Phu Nho Quan in late 1953. Finished in standard US Olive Drab, METZ was commanded by Lt. Michel Henry, a professional soldier who fought throughout Indochina; the numeral '5' denotes the leader's tank of 2nd Platoon. The registration number – French tricolor, 'IC' (signifying Indochina), '94113' – is displayed on the turret rear and on the lower hull plate, which also carries a bridge classification plate – a black '18', indicating the tank's weight in tons, on a yellow disc.

Amongst a sprawl of tents at Fire Support Base 'Rhode Island' are the main M113 variants used in Vietnam, including M106 mortar tracks, M577 command vehicles and M548 tracked load carriers, all sheltering behind RPG screens, as well as an M578 recovery vehicle. (*Armor* **Magazine)**

A2: M29C Crabe of 2e Peloton, 1er Escadron, 1er Régiment Étranger de Cavalerie; Operation 'Aquarium', Cochinchina, April 1951

After an inauspicious start when employed as an artillery supply and medical evacuation vehicle in difficult terrain, '*Crabes*' (M29C Weasels) were formed into effective fighting units by the Foreign Legion for use in the swamps and flooded paddy fields that abound in Vietnam. Operation 'Aquarium' was undertaken in the Plaine des Joncs (Plain of Reeds) west of Saigon, an area long dominated by the Viet Minh. This Crab was commanded by Adj. Blesch, the leader of 2nd Platoon (indicated by the card heart symbol) of 1st Squadron, 1st Foreign Legion Cavalry Regt. (whose unit insignia is painted on the near front quarter). On the far bow quarter is an insignia of a crab combined with a Foreign Legion grenade; its '1' cypher identifies the

An M551 Sheridan of Tp. A, 1st Sqn., 1st Cav. of the 23rd Inf. Div. 'Americal' is refuelled from an M54 5-ton truck during operations near Tam Ky, March 1970. (US Army)

1er Groupe d'escadrons du 1er REC, the tactical grouping of the regiment's 1st, 2nd and 6th Sqns. which operated the Crabs and Alligators at this date. (The insignia was later retained by the 1er and 2e Groupements Autonomes, and the 1er and 2e Groupements Amphibies, as these expanding tactical units were later renamed.)

B1: AUERSTAEDT, M24 Chaffee of Peloton Prèaud, 'Escadron de Marche du 1er Régiment de Chasseurs à Cheval'; strongpoint 'Isabelle', Dien Bien Phu, March 1954

The ten M24 tanks airlifted to Dien Bien Phu were camouflaged in various schemes of sand yellow and red ochre stripes over the Olive Drab base colour. AUERSTAEDT was commanded by Lt. Henri Prèaud, the platoon leader at strongpoint 'Isabelle' isolated to the south of the main position at Dien Bien Phu. To the troops the Chaffees were known as 'Bisons', and to the Viet Minh as 'Oxen'. They bore the names of famous battles in French military history, written in white capitals along the turret sides, which were normally used as radio callsigns. This did not apply to those at 'Isabelle' however – AUERSTAEDT, RATISBONNE and NEUMACH. Their callsigns were *Vert Un*, *Vert Deux* and *Vert Trois* respectively ('Green One', 'Two' and 'Three'). Besides the names, the only markings carried were the registration number on the lower hull front and turret rear, AUERSTAEDT being IC-94266 and the others -67 and -68. Although officially attached to 3e Escadron, 1er RCC for administrative purposes and designated 'Escadron de Marche du 1er RCC', the tank crews preferred the alternative title 'Escadron de Chars du GONO' (Groupe Opérationnel du Nord-Ouest) – the acronym being a French pun on an obvious piece of male anatomy. AUERSTAEDT was the only tank to survive the battle without serious damage: on the evening of 7 May it was destroyed by its crew when the fortress was overwhelmed by the Viet Minh.

B2: D'ARC II, M5A1 of 4e Peloton, 3e Escadron, 5e Régiment de Cuirassiers 'Royal-Pologne', Groupement Mobile 100; Poste Kilométrique 14, Route 19, Annam, 4 April 1954

The tanks of '$3^{e}/5^{e}$ Cuirs' were ancient but re-engined M5A1s. The 4e Peloton, commanded by Lt. Goldstein, comprised three M5A1 tanks, two M8 self-propelled howitzers and two M3 half-tracks. Vehicle names began with the letter D – the platoon leader's tank being DROUOT II, the other tanks D'ARC II and DE SAXE; the M8 HMCs DUROC

Despite being few in numbers, the Royal Australian Armoured Corps units of 3rd Cavalry and 1st Armd. Regts. made a significant contribution to the success of operations conducted by 1st Australian Task Force in Vietnam; here, Centurions and APCs kick up the dust while crossing a dry paddyfield during an operation in 1969. (Australian War Memorial)

and DON QUICHOTTE; and the M3 half-tracks DAGOBERT and DAMOCLÈS. D'ARC II was commanded by Maréchal-des-logis-chef (Staff Sgt.) Leopold de Temmermann, and fought a decisive action at PK14 when 4e Peloton saved from annihilation two companies of the Régiment de Corée, battle-hardened veterans of the French battalion which fought with UN forces in Korea. Along the hull sides are the registration number, tank name, and the insignia of the 'Royal-Pologne'. The registration number is repeated on the glacis plate. Also illustrated is one of the platoon's M8 Howitzer Motor Carriages bearing the name DON QUICHOTTE, an evocative name to many professional soldiers who served in Indochina. In the words of one armour officer: 'There is a difference between us French and Don Quixote. Don Quixote rode against windmills believing they were giants; we ride against windmills knowing that they are windmills, but doing it all the same, because we think that there ought to be someone in this materialistic world who rides against windmills.'

M113A1 APCs of 3 Tp., B Sqn., 3rd Cav. Regt., set up a Night Defensive Position (NDP) during an operation in Phuoc Tuy Province in 1970; the majority of Australian APCs in Vietnam were fitted with Cadillac-Gage T50 machine gun turrets. (Doug Lennox)

C1: M41A3 of 1st Squadron, 5th Armoured Cavalry Regiment, Army of the Republic of Vietnam; Da Nang, May 1966

In March 1966 civil insurrection broke out in the northern provinces of South Vietnam in what became known as the Buddhist Revolt. Government forces, including the M41A3 tanks of 5th Armd. Cav. Regt., were airlifted to Da Nang to restore control. Flown in by USAF C-133 Cargomasters from Tan Son Nhut airbase near Saigon, the tanks supported ARVN Marines and paratroopers as they crushed Buddhist resistance in the pagodas of Da Nang. This M41A3 carries the registration number '81557' in black on a yellow rectangle on the lower hull front and top rear hull plate. The red/yellow/blue bands on the gun barrel are the individual platoon colours; combined, they signify a squadron headquarters tank. The unit serial '501' in black on a white rectangle on the right front trackguard indicates the squadron commander's tank. On the opposite trackguard are the letters 'TG' in white on a red disc outlined in white – a marking carried on all ARVN AFVs, standing for Thiet Giap: 'armour command'. These markings are repeated on the rear trackguards.

C2: M50A1 Ontos of 2nd Platoon, Company B, 3rd Anti-Tank Battalion, USMC; Operation 'Deckhouse VI', I CTZ, February 1967

As part of the Special Landing Force of the Seventh Fleet operating off the coast of Vietnam, Battalion Landing Team 1/4, supported by the Ontos vehicles of 2nd Ptn., Co. B, 3rd Anti-Tank Bn., landed by 'amtracs' on 16 February near Sa Huyn at the southern tip of I Corps Tactical Zone. During Operation 'Deckhouse VI', 204 of the enemy were killed at a cost to the Marines of five dead and 55 wounded. The callsign of this Ontos, 'B-23', is displayed in white on the left front trackguard as viewed, and on the rear doors. On the opposite trackguard and on the hull sides is the 'caltrop' insignia of 3rd MARDIV, beneath which is the registration number 'USMC 226840' in chrome

yellow. The 'brothers' have named their Ontos 'Soul Tractor', which is written along the top outside tubes of the 106 mm recoilless rifles.

M577 command vehicles and M113 APCs of Task Force 255, comprising the ARVN 10th, 15th and 18th Armd. Cav. Regts., advance into the Parrot's Beak area during the Cambodian incursion of May 1970. (US Army)

D1: M48A3 Patton of Tank Section, A Company HQ, 1st Tank Battalion, USMC; Hue City, I CTZ, February 1968

In the savage street-fighting in Hue during the Tet Offensive of 1968, Ontos and Patton tanks played an important rôle in support of the Marines. This M48A3 is depicted in support of 1st Bn., 5th Marines as they fought their way, yard by yard, into the Imperial City. The vehicle number 'A-51' in white identifies the tank of 'Alpha' Co. commander. Along the 90 mm barrel is the tank name MAD HARLOT in Gothic script. The yellow shield bearing '1 TK' in black is the insignia of 1st Tank Bn., Fleet Marine Force; and on the left front trackguard as viewed is the bridge classification weight of 52 tons. Forward of the turret co-incidence rangefinder housing is a 'body count' tally of two orientals in coolie hats adorned with red stars.

D2: ACAV of Company D, 1st Squadron, 11th Armored Cavalry Regiment; Operation 'Atlas Wedge', III CTZ, March 1969

Operation 'Atlas Wedge' was conducted in the Michelin Rubber Plantation west of Lai Khe; and DRAFT DODGER was attached to the tank company of 1st Sqn., 11ACR. In order to retain an amphibious capability it is fitted with styrofoam flotation pods on the front hull plate, which compensate for the extra weight of 'belly armour' added to the hull floor to give greater protection from landmines. Besides the standard bumper codes and registration number, DRAFT DODGER is embellished with GT 'go-faster' stripes. (For other ACAV schemes in Vietnam, see Vanguard No. 34, *The M113 Series*.)

E1: M35A2 'Gun Truck' of 444th Transportation Company, 27th Transportation Battalion, 8th Transportation Group (Motor Transport); Qui Nhon, II CTZ, September 1968

US Forces in Vietnam were dispersed in bases throughout the country and, for the most part, were supplied by motor transport units operating out of major sea ports. Roads were frequently interdicted by the enemy, and 'line-haul' operations were always hazardous. Since armoured and Military Police units were not always available for convoy escort, transport groups added armour plate and multiple weapons to some of their trucks to provide

NVA T-54s lie abandoned in the streets of An Loc after the assault on Binh Long Province in April 1972; the lead tank was knocked out by a 105 mm howitzer on 13 April, while the second and third were destroyed two days later by ARVN tank-killer teams armed with M-72 LAWs. (*Armor* **Magazine**)

their own protection against ambush. NANCY is an M35A2 6×6 2½-ton Kaiser Jeep truck mounting an M55 'quad fifty' and an M60 machine gun with partial armour protection for the crew. Although effective in the rôle, such 'gun trucks' and their supporting personnel reduced the cargo-carrying capability and available manpower of transport units.

E2: M577A1 Armored Command Post Vehicle, Headquarters and HQ Troop, 2nd Squadron, 11th Armored Cavalry Regiment; Bien Hoa, III CTZ, May 1969

One of several M113 variants employed in Vietnam, the M577 acted as a command post, communications station, fire support co-ordination centre, and as a medical treatment and evacuation vehicle. The black prancing mustang on the sides of this M577A1 identifies it as belonging to 11th Armd. Cav. Regt. – the largest US armoured unit to see service in Vietnam. Acting in the command rôle with the HQ Troop of 2/11ACR, it stands by a hoarding stating the tactical principles of the Blackhorse Regiment.

F1: M42A1 Duster of Battery D, 5th Battalion (Automatic Weapon Self-Propelled), 2nd Artillery; Quan Loi, III CTZ, May 1969

Returned to active service for the Vietnam conflict, the obsolescent M42A1 Duster proved to be highly successful in a variety of rôles other than that for which it was intended, since no enemy ground-attack aircraft were encountered. Nicknamed 'Delta Dud's', Bty. D adopted the Disney cartoon character Goofy as their unit mascot; he is shown here about to step on a landmine – the cause of most AFV casualties. Across the gunshield of the dual 40 mm Bofors is the legend 'First In and the Last Out', a reflection on the regimental motto: 'The Second First'. Assigned to III Corps Tactical Zone, 5/2nd Arty. came under operational control of II Field Force Vietnam Artillery, whose insignia is displayed on the rear top hull plate (left) beside that of 2nd Artillery (right).

F2: M109 155 mm Self-Propelled Howitzer, Battery L, 4th Battalion, 12th Marines, USMC; Operation 'Chinook', I CTZ, February 1967

Designed for mobile operations in support of armoured and mechanised units in Europe, self-propelled guns in Vietnam fought predominantly from prepared positions in fire support bases and permanent encampments. With a maximum range of almost 15 kilometres, the M109 provided rapid fire support to manoeuvre units operating in the hostile countryside of the 'boonies'. This M109 of L/4/12 Marines is conducting a fire mission during Operation 'Chinook', which was intended to block enemy infiltration routes into the coastal plains and the city of Hue during the monsoon season. Besides the registration numbers 'USMC 313567' on sides and rear, the only marking displayed on this M109 is the vehicle name in Marine chrome yellow CONG BUSTER along the barrel of the 155 mm howitzer.

G1: M551 Sheridan of 1st Armored Cavalry Platoon, Troop B, 1st Squadron, 11th Armored Cavalry Regiment; An Loc, III CTZ, August 1969

From early 1969 the Sheridan began to replace some of the M48 Pattons and ACAVs in the armoured cavalry squadrons in Vietnam. Designed as 'a lightweight armored vehicle to support ground reconnaissance', the Sheridan suffered a number of problems during its initial deployment, but eventually over 200 were used in SE Asia[1]. Besides its 152 mm main armament, this M551 Sheridan of 1st Sqn., 11ACR has been given additional firepower with twin .50cal. Brownings at the commander's position and twin M73 7.62 mm machine guns at the loader's hatch. In the Blackhorse Regiment most vehicles were named

[1]For the full story of the Sheridan's troubled career, see Vanguard 40, *US Light Tanks 1944–84*.

ARVN troops withdraw through the town of Bong Son under the covering guns of an M41A3 during the final battles of 1975; by then ARVN armour units had been debilitated by a lack of fuel, ammunition and spares, and were unable to stem the onslaught of NVA tanks. (*Armor* Magazine)

beginning with the troop letter, and this Sheridan is called BODY COUNT, after that most ghoulish and morbid term of military jargon to emerge from the war, which became an actual indicator of success on the battlefield in the strategy of attrition waged by US forces in Vietnam. It also sports on the commander's gunshield the names 'The Stalking Rhino'; and 'Blood and Guts', after the regimental commander, Col. George S. Patton (July 1968–April 1969). To the front and rear it carries standard bumper codes, and on the sides the registration number.

G2: M728 Combat Engineer Vehicle of 919th Engineer Company, 11th Armored Cavalry Regiment; Quan Loi, III CTZ, May 1969

Based on the M60 Main Battle Tank, the CEV M728 full-track combat engineer vehicle replaced the tank-'dozer in divisional engineer battalions. A boom and winch are attached to the turret for lifting and carrying equipment. It is armed with a 165 mm demolition gun. A driver-operated 'dozer blade is mounted at the front. In Vietnam its powerful main armament was highly effective for perimeter defence, counter-ambush fire and against field fortifications, while its ability to smash its way through jungle earned it the nickname 'Bull of the Woods'. On one occasion it even spearheaded an infantry/cavalry charge of the 23rd Inf. Div. (Americal) in the village of Tap An Bac on 19 June 1969, when divisional elements came to the rescue of two bulldozers and a working party of the 26th Eng. Bn. under enemy attack. This M728 of 919th Eng. Co. – the 'Blackhorse's own' – displays the unit's unofficial 'devil' insignia on the turret sides. Bumper codes are carried on the arms of the A-frame boom and rear trackguards. Along the 165 mm demolition gun is painted the vehicle name 'PEACE TALK' – an ironic reference to the diplomatic posturing conducted in Paris at the time.

H1: Centurion Mark 5/1 (Aust) of 2 Troop, A Squadron, 1st Armoured Regiment, 1st Australian Task Force; Phuoc Tuy Province, III CTZ, September 1970

The only tanks other than US ones used in Vietnam by the Free World forces were the Centurions of the 1st ATF. From February 1968 to September 1971, four squadrons of 1st Armd. Regt. served in Vietnam on a rotating basis – C Sqn., followed by B, then A, and C again. For the most part they operated in Phuoc Tuy Province, east of Saigon, and the vehicle name of this Centurion Mark 5/1 (Aust) is a simple play on words to that effect, complete with Vietnamese accents and pronounced in the obvious manner, declaring the crew's assessment of the situation and the province. The registration number is carried on the top right of the glacis plate (as viewed) and at the top right of the rear auxiliary fuel tank.

The inset view shows some other vehicle names on the 20-pdr. barrels of Australian Centurions in Vietnam, most of which were somewhat crude in nature: BUKU was a Vietnamese corruption of the French word *beaucoup* (much, a lot, many); and BOOM BOOM was one of the services made available by Saigon 'tea ladies', as well as indicating the function of the weapon upon which the name is inscribed.

H2: T-59 of 203rd Armoured Regiment, North Vietnamese Army; Saigon, 30 April 1975

Maintaining a grotesque fiction to the last by flying the flag of the NLF (National Liberation Front), a Chinese-built T-59 of the NVA 203rd Armd. Regt. drives through the gates of the Doc Lap presidential palace on the fall of Saigon. By 1975 the NVA had some 600 medium tanks of the T-54/T-59 type. The markings on this T-59 are simply the vehicle number in white on the turret sides and 'B988' on the rear hull plate.

Notes sur les planches en couleur

A1 Le tank du Lt. Michel Henry est peint en *Olive drab* américain. Le '5' identifie le chef du 2e Peloton et l'insigne de régiment du 1er RCC est peint sur la tourelle. **A2** Le véhicule de l'Adjudant Blesch a un symbole en forme de coeur identifiant le chef du 2e Peloton; le symbole du régiment du 1er REC est peint du côté gauche et de l'autre côté se trouve l'enseigne du 1er groupe d'escadrons.

B1 Le tank du Lt. Prèaud présente l'un de plusieurs modèles de bandes sable et marron-rouge vues sur les 'Buffles' de Dien Bien Phu. Les seules marques sont le nom et le numéro de série. **B2** Le tank du Maréchal des logis chef Temmermann, qui eut un combat décisif pour le soutien du Régt. de Corée, porte sur le côté de coque son numéro de série, son nom, et l'insigne simplifiée du régiment *Royal-Pologne*. Un des HMC M8 du même peloton est présenté en arrière-plan.

C1 Les bandes de fût indiquent qu'il s'agit d'un tank du quartier général d'escadron; le numéro '501' le commandant d'escadron. L'insigne rouge et blanche 'TG' était portée par tous les tanks *ARVN*. **C2** Signe d'appel radio de véhicule individuel 'B-23' sur garde-boue et portes arrière; insigne en étoile à trois pointes de la *3rd Marine Division* sur les garde-boues et côtés de coque; le nom du véhicule '*Soul Tractor*' sur le fût du canon.

D1 Le numéro 'A-51' permet de reconnaître le commandant de compagnie 'A'. L'écusson jaune portant '1 TK' identifie le *1st Marine Tank Battalion*; '*Mad Harlot*' sur le fût du canon est le nom de l'équipage pour son tank; et les deux visages vietnamiens de bande dessinée sont des symboles de mort. **D2** Des abréviations des unités américaines normalisées sont peintes sur les garde-boues; '*Draft Dodger*' est le nom du véhicule de l'équipage.

E1 Véhicule d'escorte de convoie improvisé avec mitrailleuses quadruples de *0.50-calibre* et une mitrailleuse M60; le nom pittoresque a été donné par l'équipage. **E2** Le cheval grossièrement peint identifie la *11th Armored Cavalry*, le Régiment du Cheval Noir. Le signe présente la devise de cette unité, commandée par le fils du Gén. George Patton.

F1 Les insignes sont: un 'Goofy' de Walt Disney, mascotte de la Batterie D; sur la coque arrière, les insignes (à gauche) de la *11 Field Force Vietnam Artillery* et du *2nd Artillery Regt.*; et sur la protection du canon 'First In and Last Out' (premier arrivé, dernier parti). **F2** La seule insigne à part le numéro de série est le nom '*Cong Buster*' sur le fût de canon.

G1 Le nom '*Body Count*' ('Compte des cadavres') commence avec l'initiale de *Troop B*. Les slogans sont '*The Stalking Rhino*' (Le rhino d'affût') et '*Blood and Guts*' ('Sang et entrailles') rappelant le surnom du célèbre père du commandant du régiment. **G2** '*Peace Talk*' ('Entretien pour la paix') – nom ironique s'il en fut – porte sur la tourelle l'écusson de 'diable' de la *919th Engineer Company*, rattachée à la *11th Armored Cavalry*.

H1 Le nom qui se trouve sur le canon est un jeu de mots sur le nom de la province et sur une phrase populaire mais qui ne peut pas être imprimée. D'autres exemples des noms donnés aux *Centurions* australiens sont présentés dans les illustrations de détail. **H2** Ce tank est celui qui entra dans le palais présidentiel de Doc Lap à Saïgon durant le dernier jour de cette longue guerre. Il porte toujours de façon trompeuse un drapeau du *Viet Cong* plutôt qu'un drapeau nord-vietnamien.

Farbtafeln

A1 Der Panzer von Lt. Michel Henry ist in US-*Olive Drab* gestrichen. An der '5' erkennt man den Führer des *2e Peloton*, und die Insignien des Regiments, des 1er RCC, befinden sich am Geschützturm. **A2** An *Adjudant* Bleschs Fahrzeug befindet sich ein herzförmiges Symbol, an dem man den Führer des *2e Peloton* erkennt. Auf dieser Seite sieht man das Regimentszeichen des 1er REC, und auf der anderen Seite das der *1er Groupe d'escadrons*.

B1 An Lt. Prèauds Panzer sehen Sie ein Beispiel der vielen verschiedenen sandfarbenen/rotbraunen Streifenschemen, die man auf den 'Buffaloes' (Büffeln) von Dien Bien Phu fand. Name und Seriennummer sind die einzige Markierung. **B2** Der Panzer von Oberfeldwebel Temmermann, der das *Régt. de Corée* erfolgreich unterstützte, hat auf den Geschützseiten seine Seriennummer sowie Namen und vereinfachte Insignien des '*Royal-Pologne*'-Regiments. Im Hintergrund sehen Sie einen M8 HMCs desselben Zugs.

C1 An den Geschützrohrstreifen erkennt man einen Panzer des Hauptquartiers der Schwadron. Die Nummer '501' bezeichnet den Schwadronskommandanten. Alle *ARVN*-Panzer hatten die rot-weissen Insignien 'TG'. **C2** Auf dem Kettenschutz und den Türen hinten sehen Sie das Radio-Rufzeichen 'B-23' dieses Fahrzeugs. Auf den Geschützseiten und dem anderen Kettenschutz sind die Insignien der *3rd Marine Division* in Form eines dreizackigen Sterns zu sehen. Das Geschützrohr trägt den Namen '*Soul Tractor*'.

D1 Die Nummer 'A-51' bezeichnet den Kommandanten der A-Kompanie. Am gelben Schild mit der Aufschrift '1 TK' erkennt man das *1st Marine Tank Battalion*. Die Besatzung dieses Panzers hat das Fahrzeug '*Mad Harlot*' genannt, wie man am Lauf sieht. Die beiden Karikaturen vietnamesischer Gesichter symbolisieren das Motto 'Töten'. **D2** Die üblichen abgekürzten Bezeichnungen amerikanischer Einheiten sind auf dem Kettenschutz zu sehen. Das Fahrzeug trägt den Namen '*Draft Dodger*'.

E1 Improvisiertes Eskortenfahrzeug mit vier *.50-calibre* Maschinengewehren und einem M60 Maschinengewehr. Die Besatzung wählte diesen einfallsreichen Namen. **E2** Der Umriss des Pferdes bezeichnet die *11th Armored Cavalry*, das 'Black Horse Regiment' (Regiment mit dem Schwarzen Pferd). Auf dem Schild sehen Sie das Motto dieser Einheit, deren Kommandant der Sohn General George S. Pattons ist.

F1 Das Maskottchen der D-Batterie ist Walt Disneys 'Goofy'. Hinten am Rumpf sind die Abzeichen der *II Field Force Vietnam Artillery* (links) und des *2nd Artillery Regt.* zu sehen, und am Geschütz der Slogan 'First In and Last Out' (Zuerst herein und zuletzt heraus). **F2** Ausser der Seriennummer ist die einzige Markierung der Name '*Cong Buster*' am Geschützrohr.

G1 Der Name '*Body Count*' beginnt mit dem Anfangsbuchstaben der *Troop B*. Andere Slogans wie '*The Stalking Rhino*' und '*Blood and Guts*' rühren vom Spitznamen des berühmten Vaters vom Regimentskommandanten her. **G2** Dieser Panzer, der ironischerweise den Namen *Peace Talk* hat, ist am Geschütz mit dem 'Teufels'-Abzeichen der *919th Engineer Company* versehen, die der *11th Armored Cavalry* angegliedert war.

H1 Der Name am Geschütz ist vom Namen der Provinz und von einer beliebten Redewendung, die wir besser nicht aufführen, abgeleitet. Andere Beispiele von Namen für die australischen *Centurions* finden Sie auf den Einzelabbildungen. **H2** Das ist der Panzer, der am letzten Tag des langen Krieges in den Präsidentenpalast Doc Lap in Saigon fuhr. Angeblich hatte er eine '*Viet Cong*'-Flagge und keine nordvietnamesische.